Stones&Cones

Jillian Hulme Gilliland • Mary Alice Downie

Scholastic-TAB Publications Ltd.,
123 Newkirk Road, Richmond Hill, Ontario, Canada

Canadian Cataloguing in Publication Data

Downie, Mary Alice, 1934-
  Cones & stones

Also issued in French under title: Artisan de la nature.
ISBN 0-590-71227-6

1. Nature craft – Juvenile literature.   I. Gilliland,
Jillian Hulme, 1943-   II. Title.

TT873.D67 1984   j745.5   C83-099235-9

1st printing 1984   Printed in Canada
2nd printing 1984

For Margaret Fletcher

Contents

Safety note: Whenever you see this symbol *, you should ask an adult to help you, since the material or tool needed might be difficult to work with.

Substitutions: If any of the seeds or plants or other natural materials aren't readily available, just use another seed or cone which has a similar shape.

The
Forgotten
Ark

Dandy-Lion

You will need: a large dandelion on its stem, 7 dead dandelion flower tops (5 on their stems), long green twist ties, 3 dark twigs 0.6 cm long, 2 straight pins, scissors

1. For the body, lay out stems like this:

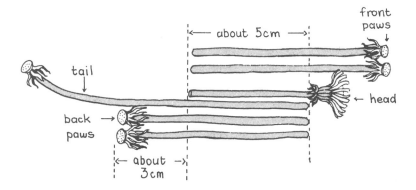

2. Bind stems together with twist ties, finishing off between front legs.

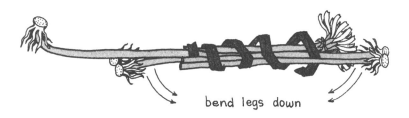

bend legs down

3. For the face, snip dry tops and sepals (the section below the flower head) off two dead flower heads. Pin the round parts onto the lower part of the large dandelion face to form whisker pads.

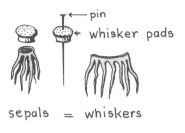

sepals = whiskers

4. Push the cut-off sepals behind the pads to make whiskers.

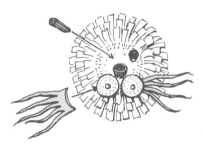

5. Push 2 small twigs into the top of the face for eyes. Push 1 larger twig above the whisker pads for the nose.

Bunny Willows

You will need: pussywillows, peanuts (in shells), contact glue* or white school glue, a felt pen

1. To make the mother bunny, select a long peanut for the body. Glue a round peanut head on the narrow end, and let dry. (If the bunny won't stand up, ask an adult to pry the peanut out of the head and to glue the head back together.*)

pussywillows

2. Glue on pussywillows for ears, paws and tail, in the order shown.

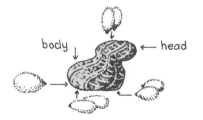

body ↓   ← head

3. To make each baby bunny, select a "double" peanut or glue two round peanuts together.

4. Glue on pussywillows in the order shown to make ears, tail, front and back paws.

5. Draw on the eyes and nose with felt pen.

Acorn Squirrels

1. For the body, stand acorn on wider end. Glue on spruce cone for tail and 2 watermelon seeds for paws.

Ironwood tree pods (or any large seeds like pumpkin pips)

larch cone

spruce cones

acorns

2. For the head, glue the tamarack cone to the top of the acorn. Push hornbeam or ironwood pods behind 1 row of cone scales to make ears. Glue. Draw on eyes, nose and mouth with felt pen.

Spruce Cone Bees

You will need: a white spruce cone, small acorns still in their cups, 2 sugar maple keys, white school glue, 2 maple key stems, a black felt pen

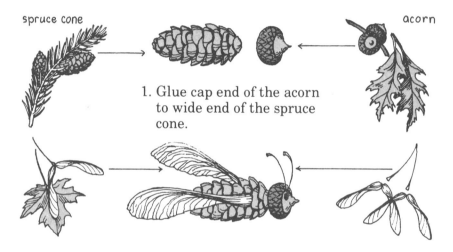

spruce cone

acorn

1. Glue cap end of the acorn to wide end of the spruce cone.

2. Put a dab of glue on the thick end of 2 maple keys. Push well in between the cone scales, behind the head, for wings.

3. Glue maple key stems to acorn, knobby end out, for feelers.

4. Draw on eyes with felt pen.

Cattail Dragonflies

You will need: a cattail, large peppercorns or 2 small black buttons or 2 large black beads, 4 maple keys, white school glue

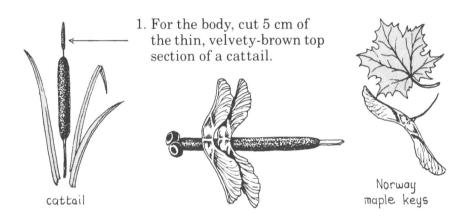

1. For the body, cut 5 cm of the thin, velvety-brown top section of a cattail.

cattail

Norway maple keys

2. Glue 2 peppercorns, buttons or beads to the wider end for eyes.

3. Glue 2 pairs of maple keys to the back, near the head, for wings.

Note: If you want to suspend your creatures, just tie on some thread and hang them up.

Walnut Animals

Mice

You will need: empty walnut shells, contact glue* or white school glue, pins, a needle, thread, scissors, paper, peppercorns, a pencil, brown felt

1. Trace ear pattern onto paper. Pin to felt and cut out. Repeat for the second ear.

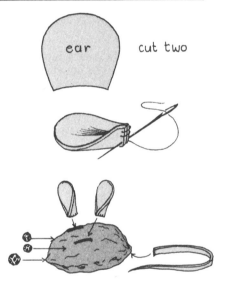

ear   cut two

2. Fold ear in half as shown and oversew straight edges together.

3. Make 2 equally-spaced marks on top of walnut, a third of the distance from the pointed end of the shell. Glue ears along marks, with the cupped part forward.

4. Glue on peppercorns for eyes and nose.

5. Glue a felt strip, 8 cm long, under the back of the shell for a tail.

Turtles

You will need: S-shaped pieces of styrofoam from packing boxes, black and brown felt pens, empty walnut shells, contact glue* or white school glue, sunflower seeds

1. Colour an S-shaped piece of styrofoam with brown felt pen. Draw on black eyes, nostrils and mouth.

2. Glue head onto rounded end of walnut shell, pressing the styrofoam-piece up under the front of the walnut shell as shown.

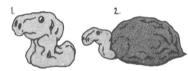

3. Glue pointed ends of sunflower seeds under shell edge for legs, 2 facing forward and 2 facing backward.

4. Pattern shell with black felt pen. First draw a square in the middle, then a ring of pie shapes and a row of scallops around the rim.

You can even put a marble under the shells of your walnut animals and race them down a tipped tray.

Pine Cone Owls

You will need: 2 small pine cones, Hazelnut shells, lima beans, watermelon seeds, acorn caps, maple keys, beechnut pod sections, felt, felt pen, bristol board or heavy paper, contact glue* or white school glue

1. Stand larger cone on flat end for body.

2. Push smaller cone sideways onto its top for the head, leaving a piece of stem for the beak. Glue together.

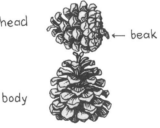

head

← beak

body

3. For eyes, wings and feet, use any of the ideas below. Glue the pieces on, or push them well in between the pine cone scales and glue into place.

acorn cups

beechnut pods

pine cone scales

Hazelnuts

A: EYES: circles of black, white and yellow felt glued together

EARS, WINGS, FEET: large pine cone scales

B: EYES: white bristol board
CAP: acorn cap
WINGS: maple keys
FEET: beechnut pod sections

C: EYES: lima beans drawn upon with felt pen
WINGS: split Hazelnut shell
FEET: watermelon seeds

11

Pebble Pets

You will need: pebbles (both large and small) with pretty and unusual colours and interesting shapes, contact glue* or white school glue, cotton balls, poster paints and paintbrushes or felt pens, clear nail polish

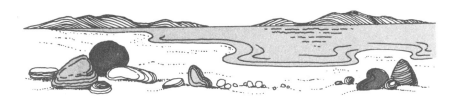

1. Glue the smaller stones to the larger ones to make some of the creatures opposite. Let glue dry. For eye stalks or bird's combs, glue small pebbles together first, and allow to dry before attaching to heads. (You may need to support the pebbles with books or boxes while glue is drying.) Use cotton balls soaked in glue between large stones.

cotton
balls
soaked
in glue

eye stalks

2. When glue is dry, paint or draw on features and markings.

3. When paint is dry, varnish with nail polish.

snail

frog

birds

toadstools

ladybirds

beaver

turtle

13

Burr Beasties

1. Start with a body of several burrs and add head, legs, tail, neck and ears. Simply press the prickly brown burrs against one another to make them stick.

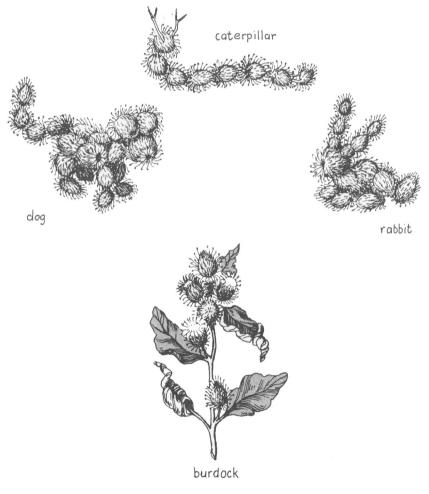

caterpillar

dog

rabbit

burdock

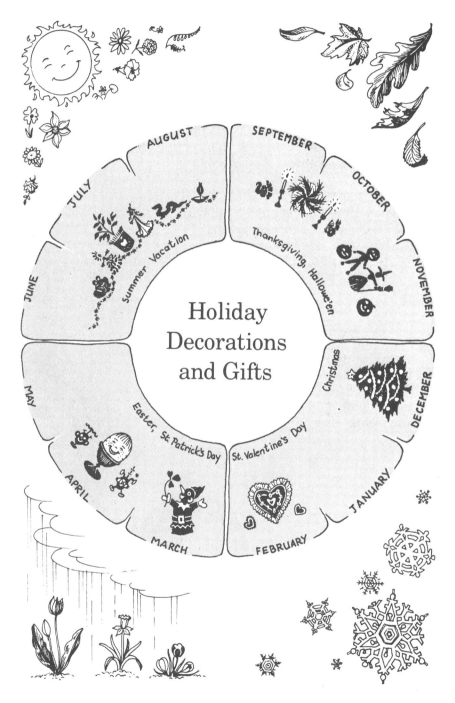

Holiday
Decorations
and Gifts

AUGUST
SEPTEMBER
OCTOBER
JULY
NOVEMBER
JUNE
DECEMBER
MAY
JANUARY
APRIL
FEBRUARY
MARCH

Summer Vacation
Thanksgiving, Halloween
Christmas
St. Valentine's Day
Easter, St. Patrick's Day

Saint Valentine's Day

Long ago, Valentine greetings were all made by hand. People painted them or made cut-out hearts and flowers and glued them onto hearts and cards. On Valentine's Day we still like to give and receive flowers. It is said that when he was in prison, St. Valentine himself was given little bunches of flowers by the children who loved him.

You will need: coloured cardboard, white school glue, scissors, needle, thread, scraps of lace, pressed or dried flowers (e.g., everlastings or rice flowers. Lace flowers or cut-outs will do, too, or you can paint or draw them yourself.), paper

1. Cut out a large cardboard heart. (Make a paper pattern first and trace it onto the card.) Draw a faint line down the centre of the heart. This helps keep your work even.

cardboard

paper

16

2. Arrange the lace around the heart and on it to make a pleasant pattern. You can gather it by making small stitches along the straight edge of the lace, then drawing the thread tighter.

3. Squeeze a thin line of glue onto the heart where you want your lace to lie. Put lace on top, cover with paper and press under a book until dry.

4. Arrange the flowers on the heart. Squeeze glue onto the backs of the flowers and replace.

5. Hang up your heart using thread or ribbon.

Potato Puppets for St. Patrick's Day

You'll have all the luck of the Irish with this jolly little leprechaun.

> **To make his head you will need:** a large potato, a big carrot, a piece of celery, a green pepper or chili, 2 cloves, toothpicks, an apple corer*

1. Ask an adult to make a hole with the coring knife, in one end of the potato, big enough to put your finger into.

2. Fasten the puppet's eyes, ears, nose, mouth and cap with pieces of toothpicks. (Use the pointed ends.) If you need a point at both ends (e.g., for the carrot nose) ask an adult to cut the toothpick at a slant.

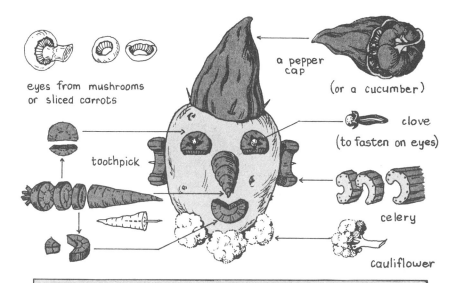

eyes from mushrooms or sliced carrots

a pepper cap

(or a cucumber)

clove
(to fasten on eyes)

toothpick

celery

cauliflower

> **To make the body you will need:** green felt (17 cm x 35 cm or big enough to cover your spread-out hand), pink felt for hands, black felt (or fabric) for belt, gold paper (or felt) for buckle, scissors, needle, green thread, white school glue

1. Fold felt in half as shown.

2. Cut a *tiny* hole at the top for the tip of your finger.

3. Shape sleeves and sides as shown and cut out. Snip sleeve ends in little points.

4. Trace this glove and cut out 2 from pink felt. Fasten inside sleeve ends with a dab of glue.

5. Sew or glue seams together.

6. Cut a circle from scraps of green felt. Snip edges as shown and glue around neck.

7. Cut a strip of black felt 1 cm wide. Glue around middle for a belt.

8. Cut a 2-cm square of gold paper or felt, cut out a smaller square in its centre and glue over belt for a buckle.

9. Cut 2 green strips 12 cm long. Snip edges as shown and glue below belt.

10. Fit the body over your hand and place puppet's head on your finger.

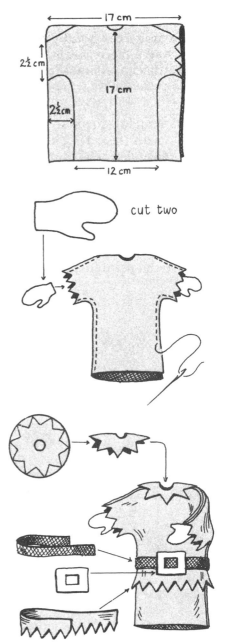

cut two

Peter Rabbit's Breakfast Table

On Easter morning, make your breakfast table cheerful with spring flowers and coloured eggs. Branches of bushes such as forsythia, lilac or apple will flower early if you cut them a week or two before Easter and bring them indoors. Pound the end of the stem with a hammer or piece of heavy wood, then stand in plenty of water. Spray the buds and stems with water every day.

When you're having soft-boiled eggs for breakfast and the eggs are cooked, use felt pens to draw the face and hair of each member of your family onto his or her egg as it sits in its egg cup. (If you turn the egg upside down to open it, the face will stay unbroken and you can keep the empty egghead shell.)

Eggniks

Eggniks live on Eggmars and come to visit Earthlings at Easter, when they can sneak in unnoticed with the chocolate eggs. A bowl full of these eggniks looks very pretty on your Easter table.

You will need: hardboiled eggs, white school glue, as many kinds of macaroni or pasta as you can find in the kitchen, paints (spray or water), paintbrush, pencil

types of macaroni

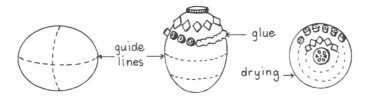

guide lines

glue

drying →

1. Begin at the top or middle of the egg and work in circles, gluing on rows of different kinds of macaroni. (Mark the middle of the egg with your pencil.) Do only a part of each egg at a time and let the glue dry, or the pieces will fall off as you turn the egg.

the egg painted

the macaroni painted

the egg and the macaroni spray painted

2. You can paint the egg *before* beginning to glue, in a strong colour such as black or red, which shows up the natural pasta colour well. Or you can paint the pasta with watercolours after it has been stuck in place, or spray paint the whole egg when finished.

23

Seed Discs

1. Glue felt over cardboard.

2. Thread needle with yarn and push it through cardboard about 0.6 cm in from the edge. Make a loop about 7 cm long and knot it.

3. Starting in the centre, arrange seeds and nuts. Glue down.

4. You can also sprinkle the disks with glitter after brushing them with glue, or spray lightly with gold or silver spray paint.

5. Hang discs from plants, cup hooks, Christmas trees and so on.

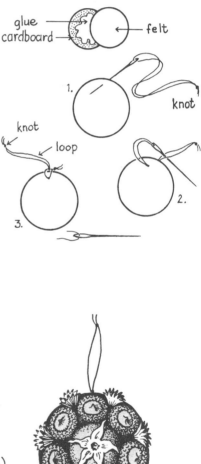

A berry (eg. Hawthorn) surrounded by small acorns and dried flowers

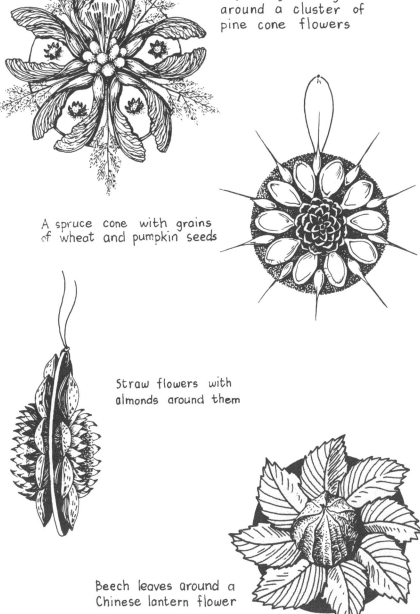

Maple keys and grass heads around a cluster of pine cone flowers

A spruce cone with grains of wheat and pumpkin seeds

Straw flowers with almonds around them

Beech leaves around a Chinese lantern flower

Wheat Wheel

You will need: about 20 heads of ripe wheat, about 50 cm of gold or yellow thread or string, 2 small gold doilies, white school glue, scissors, gold spray paint (if you like)

1. Glue doilies back to back with string ends placed between, making a 4-cm loop.

2. Arrange half the wheat heads on one side in a circle and glue down. When dry, turn over and glue remaining wheat on other side.

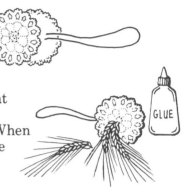

3. To spray, put wheat wheel in a cardboard box, outside or in a garage, and spray into the box.

4. Hang wheat wheel up in a doorway, window or archway.

Pine Cone Turkeys

You will need: round pine cones with flat bases, red construction paper, white school glue, scissors, a pencil

glue

leave open

1. Trace 2 turkey heads onto construction paper and cut out. Glue 2 pieces together, leaving 1 cm at the bottom open. Draw markings and features on either side of head.

2. Cut away a ring of scales near the cone's base to make a fan tail.

3. Lay the cone on its side and glue the open ends of the neck onto small scales at each side of the front of the cone.

Cornhusk Witches and Pumpkinheads

Make this unusual decoration for your Hallowe'en party table. Ask an adult to cut the top off a small pumpkin. Scrape out the seeds and fill with autumn leaves. Arrange the dolls around it, one for each guest to take home afterwards.

You will need: *dry* corn husks (soak in water before using), a *small* orange, a black felt pen, small twigs, scissors, white school glue, a knife*

To make the heads:

1. Ask an adult to cut a hole in the bottom of the orange and loosen the pulp with a knife. Scrape out with a teaspoon.

2. Draw a mouth, nose and eyes. Ask an adult to cut these out.

3. Put orange head in a warm and dry location to dry out.

To make the pumpkinhead:

1. Tear a cornhusk into strips for ties.

2. Roll 2 or 3 smaller husks together. Cut ends straight and tie each about 1 cm in from ends. These are the arms and hands.

3. Fold 3 or 4 large husks in half. Tie 2 cm down from fold. This forms the head.

4. Push arms up between husks under head and tie around the waist.

5. Divide husks below waist in two and tie ends to make legs and feet. Trim evenly. Finish off by putting the hollow orange over his head.

To make the witch: Follow steps 1 to 4 above.

corn silk

6. Cut cornhusks evenly along bottom to form a skirt. Draw face with felt pen and glue on corn silk for hair if you like.

7. Make a broom for the witch by tying a bunch of small twigs to one end of a big twig.

8. To make witch's hat cut a circle from a large cornhusk. Flatten it under a book until dry. Cut a hole in the middle. Roll up another husk to make a cone and push it through the hole in the circle. Squeeze some glue around the circle where the two pieces join and stuff cone with husks to keep the shape until dry.

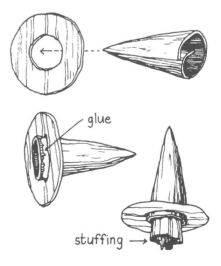

glue

stuffing →

Christmas Centrepieces

Round

You will need: a hoop of stiff cardboard 20 cm across, red or green felt the same size as the circle, white school glue, animals from the Forgotten Ark section, dried flowers and grasses, cones, nuts, seeds

```
        ←———— 20 cm ————→

                  ←10cm→          ——— felt

cardboard ——→
```

1. Glue the cardboard and felt circles together. Press under a book until glue dries.

2. Arrange animals plus dried leaves, flowers, grasses, cones, nuts and seeds. Glue into place.

Miniature Pine Cone Christmas Tree

You will need: a large pine cone, a cardboard circle about the size of the pine cone's base, dried grasses, white school glue

1. Glue broad end of pine cone to circle of cardboard.

2. Dip stem ends of dried grasses in glue and push between pine cone scales. Allow glue to dry.

Popcorn Balls and Chains

Your Christmas tree will look especially nice if you decorate it with these.

Chains

You will need: a large bowl of plain popcorn, a small bowl of cranberries, dark green thread, scissors, needle

1. Thread a needle with a very long double thread. At knotted end, make a loop 5 cm long to attach the chain to the tree branch.

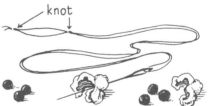

2. Thread popcorn and cranberries alternately. (Carefully push the needle through the softer, white parts of the popcorn rather than the harder kernel.)

Balls

You will need: thin red velvet ribbon or white thread, food colouring (if you like), syrup* (250 mL sugar dissolved in 125 mL water)

1. Make the syrup. Ask an adult to boil sugar and water for 5 to 10 minutes, or until quite clear. Cool 15 minutes. Add food colouring.

2. Put a handful of popcorn into a large bowl. Drizzle about 15 mL of syrup over corn and quickly form it into a ball with your hands. If syrup hardens before you can make the next ball, ask an adult to re-heat it to soften it. Cool again.

3. When balls are set, tie a ribbon or thread around the middle and make a loop for hanging it on the tree.

thread for making loop

knot

loop

35

Silver Cones

You will need: string (gold, silver, green or red), silver spray or glue and glitter, a large cardboard box, scissors, thread, straight pins, small beads, a needle, teasel heads and all sorts of pine and spruce cones

1. Tie a 15-cm piece of string around the stem or under the top scales of the teasels and larger cones. Knot ends to make a loop.

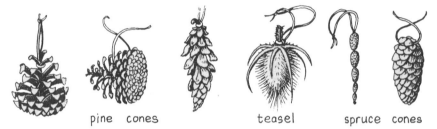

pine cones   teasel   spruce cones

2. To make a spruce "icicle," tie a bead to some thread. Thread needle and push it through the cones, working from small cones to large.

3. To spray: Attach the cones by their strings to the edge of the box with straight pins so that they hang down inside. Turn cones to make sure you spray all sides. (Work outside or in a well-ventilated room.)

Plants
& Playthings

Dandelion Chains

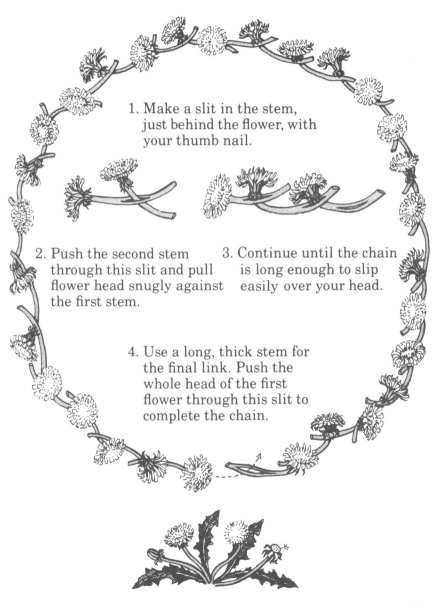

1. Make a slit in the stem, just behind the flower, with your thumb nail.

2. Push the second stem through this slit and pull flower head snugly against the first stem.

3. Continue until the chain is long enough to slip easily over your head.

4. Use a long, thick stem for the final link. Push the whole head of the first flower through this slit to complete the chain.

Leis

You will need: flowers such as petunias and phlox (or any other flower with the same round, hollow shape), a needle, thread

1. String flowers behind one another on a long piece of thread. Tie ends together when lei is long enough to slip easily over your head.

2. Or, tie together a small bunch of flowers and leaves with thread. Wrap the thread around the stems, adding more flowers as you go. Tie ends of thread together.

phlox

Daisy Crown

1. Hold daisy A sideways. Place B, upright, behind it.

2. Twist stem of daisy B up and over stem of A as shown, and behind its own flower.

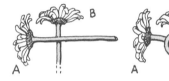 

3. Place daisy C behind the first two stems and repeat instruction 2 until the crown is long enought to sit on top of your head.

4. Push the last stems in behind the head of daisy A. Weave in a few more daisies around the crown if you like.

a crown of Queen Anne's lace

and daisies

a bracelet of vetches

and clover

Seed Necklaces

You will need: food colouring in egg cups or small containers, paper towels, pumpkin or squash seeds, a needle, thread or nylon line, small macaroni, short pieces of sumac or willow twigs, other soft seeds, slotted spoon, newspapers

1. Wash seeds and dry on paper towel. (Place newspapers under paper towel to protect table or counter-top.)

2. Place in container of food colouring and let stand half an hour.

3. Scoop seeds out with a slotted spoon and dry on a paper towel. Continue for other colours.

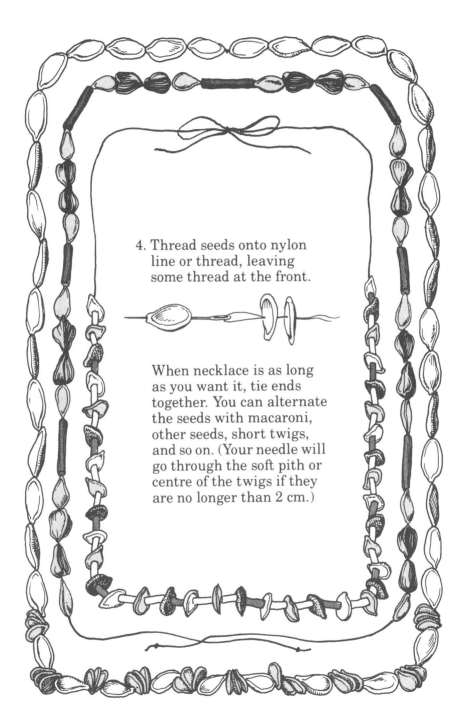

4. Thread seeds onto nylon
   line or thread, leaving
   some thread at the front.

When necklace is as long
as you want it, tie ends
together. You can alternate
the seeds with macaroni,
other seeds, short twigs,
and so on. (Your needle will
go through the soft pith or
centre of the twigs if they
are no longer than 2 cm.)

Flower Fairies

Petunia Doll

You will need: a petunia, a grape for a head, 2 twigs or thorns, a geranium flower, a geranium leaf, Queen Anne's Lace, a yarrow flowerhead

1. Pull Queen Anne's lace stem up inside petunia as shown to make a frilly petticoat.

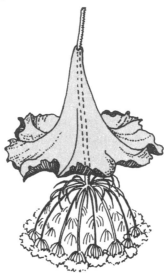

Queen Anne's lace

petunia

2. Push stem through grape and cut off.

3. Push twig arms into base of grape and put on geranium-leaf cloak.

4. Add yarrow for hair and a geranium-flower hat.

geranium

yarrow

Daisy Doll

1. Make 1 twist tie into a Z shape. Attach a second tie to the middle bar of the Z. This makes the feet.

2. Starting with the largest daisy, push the second twist tie up through its centre. Continue to the smallest daisy. Push daisies tightly against each other to form the skirt.

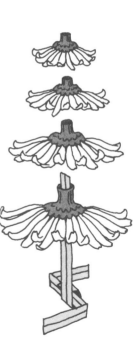

daisy

46

3. Cut the bud, leaving 0.5 cm of stem. Push on, stem first, above skirt, for bodice.

4. Tie on third twist tie for arms and push on white flowers for sleeves.

5. Pull one-third of the petals from a large daisy. This is the doll's head and bonnet. Bend 0.5 cm of body twist tie and push into the back of the flower.

6. A large daisy on its stem fastened to the doll's hand makes her parasol.

tube-shaped flower

Driftwood Delights

Driftwood can be used with dried flower arrangements or as a paperweight. A flat base is best. Vegetable oil brushed onto the finished work preserves the wood and deepens the colour.

Glue shape onto a flat base   or   smooth base with sandpaper

Driftwood Mobile

You will need: thread and string, small picture-hook eyes, a large cup hook or eye screw, a large piece of driftwood with several branches, smaller pieces of driftwood

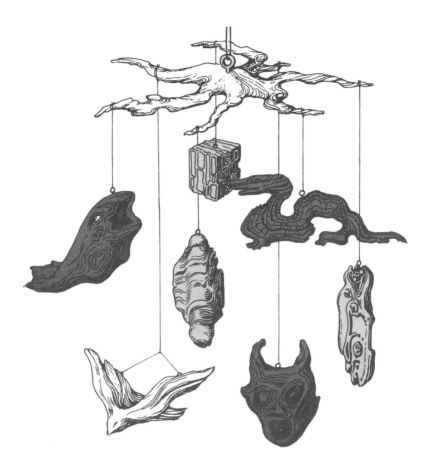

1. Screw the cup hook into the middle of the large piece of driftwood.

2. Screw a picture-hook eye into each small piece of driftwood.

3. Tie one end of the thread to the eye of the picture hook. Tie the other end around a branch of the large piece of driftwood. Use threads of different lengths so that driftwood pieces do not bump into one another.

4. Suspend the mobile by a string from a hook in the ceiling. (Ask an adult for help.)

Indoor Gardens

Plants are the main ingredients for indoor gardens, but first you will need containers for your plants.

string   fabric   fringed burlap

popsicle sticks

straws   wool   split clothes pegs

Terrific Tin Cans

You will need: empty tin cans of any size or shape but smooth around the open edge*, string or material or popsicle sticks, white school glue, scissors, a tape measure or string and ruler

Stick-covered Cans

1. Choose a can without a rim, or a milk carton or styrofoam cup.

2. Cover with popsicle sticks or straws. Secure these with a rubber band while gluing so the sticks won't slip.

milk carton

String-covered Cans

1. Choose the colours of string or yarn you want to use.

2. Spread glue over about 2.5 cm of the can at a time.

3. Wrap string or wool round and round, changing colours as you go.

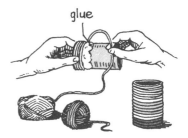

Fabric-covered Cans

1. Cut a piece of fabric as high as the can and wide enough to wrap around. (Use the tape or string to measure the can and fabric.)

2. Glue around the top and bottom edges of the can and where the fabric joins. Smooth the fabric onto the can.

3. Wrap with an old cloth or stocking until the glue is dry. If the fabric is plain, like burlap, glue on felt cut-outs and fringe the top.

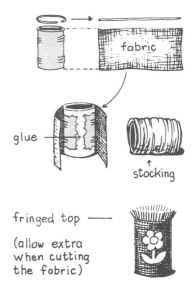

All pots need holes in the bottom for drainage. Ask an adult to hammer a few nail holes in the bottom, and stand your pot on an old saucer or plastic lid to avoid spilling water.

51

Plants from Vegetable Tops

1. Leave 1 cm of vegetable attached to the tops.

2. Place top in a small glass or plastic container three-quarters filled with small pebbles.

3. Fill bowl with water and top up daily, then watch as the pretty leaves unfurl.

Note: For a pineapple, leave 2 cm of fruit attached but ask an adult to cut away some of the outer edge. Let dry for 2 to 3 days, root in water and transplant to soil.

carrot

beetroot

radish

Plants from Fruit Seeds

You will need: seeds from any fruit (lemons, cherries, grapes, apples, grapefruit, oranges, pears, and so on), containers (from page 50), potting soil, stones or pebbles, plastic wrap or plastic bags, elastic bands

water melon
grapes
apple
pear
lemon
mandarin
cherries
plum
date and pip
peach
orange

1. Save the fruit seeds.

2. Soak them in water for a couple of hours to soften the skins.

3. Put stones or pebbles in the bottom of the containers and fill almost to the top with potting soil.

4. Push 2 or 3 seeds into the soil. (Only 1 might sprout.) Water gently.

54

5. Cover top of container with plastic wrap or a plastic bag held on by an elastic band. Remove plastic when shoots appear.

6. Place plants in a warm, light area and keep well-watered. (The plants will look lovely, but don't expect to eat the fruit, which will not appear for many years!)

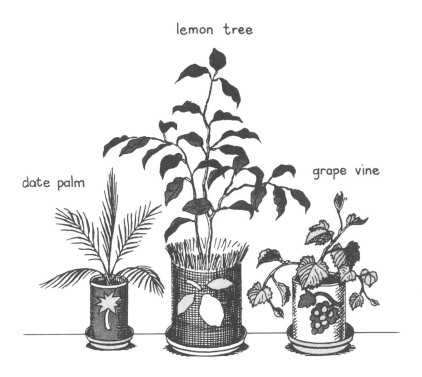

lemon tree

date palm

grape vine

A cutout on the container is a handy reminder of which pips you planted!

Vines from Yams

You will need: a yam (sweet potato) with plenty of "eyes" or buds, toothpicks, a glass jar with a mouth wider than the yam, potting soil

1. Ask an adult to cut one end off the yam.

2. Push 3 toothpicks into it, evenly spaced around the middle.

3. Rest the toothpicks on the top edge of the jar.

4. Fill the jar with water and top up as needed.

5. In about a week small pink shoots and white roots will appear. When the shoots are 2.5 cm long, plant the yam in a large pot of potting soil, covering it completely. Keep it warm and well-watered.

Note: You can do this with the seed of an avocado, too.

DRIED FLOWER GIFTS

Dried Grass Plaque

You will need: a piece of 2.5-cm thick styrofoam the size you want your plaque to be, plain material (such as burlap) 10 cm wider and higher than the styrofoam, straight pins with large heads, white school glue, a brush, yarn, paper and dried grasses

1. Centre the styrofoam on the fabric. (Dark fabric is best to show up the light grasses.) Turn edges up and pin down as shown, folding the corners neatly.

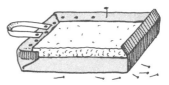

2. Pin on loop of yarn for hanger.

3. Arrange the grasses to form the desired design. Remove 1 stem at a time, brush glue onto the grass stem and head, then press in place on fabric with a tissue. Repeat for all stems.

4. Allow glue to dry thoroughly before hanging plaque up.

Flower Plaque

1. Choose a background fabric to show up the colours of your flowers. Make plaque base as on page 58.

2. Arrange flowers carefully, placing the larger ones in the middle.

3. Poke pins through flower centres to hold them in place. Glue on cones, seeds and leaves.

4. Allow glue to dry thoroughly before hanging plaque up.

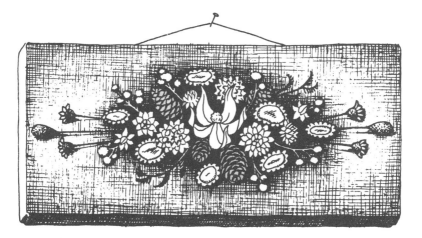

Bathtub Boats

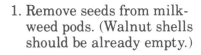

You will need: milkweed pods or empty walnut shells, paper, scissors, toothpicks, plasticine

milkweed pods

1. Remove seeds from milk-weed pods. (Walnut shells should be already empty.)

2. Push a lump of plasticine into the bottom.

3. Make a paper sail with a toothpick for a mast, as shown.

4. Push the bottom of the toothpick into the lump of plasticine.

seeds

pod

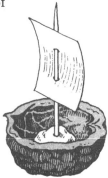

Leaf Yachts

You will need: leaves, twigs

1. Weave a thin, long twig through the middle of a large leaf, to make a sail.

2. Push the bottom of the twig through another large leaf so that half the twig sticks out below to balance the sail.

Pebble Paperweights

1. Start at one end of the pebble, or in the middle, and heavily crayon a stripe of colour. Polish with the soft rag.

2. Colour the next area and polish. Continue until the whole pebble is covered with stripes or circles of different widths of colour.

63